Feeding the Light

Jaki Shelton Green

Jaki Shelton green

Cover art: Al Johnson (**aljohnsonartstudio.com**)
Cover & interior design: Daniel Krawiec
Author Photo: Sylvia Freeman

Jacar Press
6617 Deerview Trail
Durham, NC 27712
www.jacarpress.com

Contents

Feeding the Light

daughters of this dust

i

feeling real good
big boned
mahogany ass shelf
indigo left eye
same eye grandma found
rolling around in the cat's bowl
i teach geometry from unshaven armpits
geography begins between my toes
five different patois sing your name backwards.

ii

dawn colors my back mauve
you mistake it for argentina
shipwrecked soul
you pierce me with the knives of hunger
i cry a shark's song
for the loneliness at the bottom
of your eyes.

iii

impregnating condensed light
weaving new pigmentation
into right eye.

iv

only you believed the blue eye
when she said she swam with mermaids
danced calypso beneath the sand
removed oshun curses.

v

your palms peel back my eyes
and stone the devils
living there.

waiting for love

alone cold mint tea in orange plastic torn djelaba a red
you forbid waiting drowning in six too many capsules of
magic trying to remember the words of the astrologer or
what you were screaming as you fled into the secret clay
wall of your brother's house trying to understand that i am
only allowed to pray on wednesdays pray only in the blue
mosque in Mazar-e-Sharif or join your sisters at Karte-
e-Shakhi this strange but magical Kabul my captor Kabul
the first time i drank the darkness of a particular Pashtun
male the morning i am face to face with Malalai the only
female police in Kandahar we play burqa eye games before
she slaps me shouting to lower my gaze cover my hennaed
wrists or wake up dead i return to these walls i name home
to the sacred stitches and colors rugs from your tribe my
dowry my art i smoke the ancient hashish i found buried
beneath the kitchen wall tiles your youngest sister Selah
arrives tells me it belonged to your grandmother we smoke
sleep cry eat the feta olives grapes and dream of weddings
hair beaches nail polish dark warriors bearing Tibetan music
we arrive by caravan to the wedding site your father tells
me you will come so i search for you amongst the men
that encircle the wedding party and begin wishing that i
could place a hidden camera in the back of my burqa so
i can see you when you remain invisible i am the foreign
woman laughing undetected beneath my blue wedding
tent a gift from your mother reminding me that this is the
way for a refugee wife suddenly i smell the secret blend
of wedding oils against my face it is Zarah your sister
laughing far too openly amongst men hugging thanking me
for her happiness not understanding the smile in her eyes
i do not feel my body shift or her left hand seize the gun
from my pocket Zarah my sister-in-law forced to marry

the man with green teeth shoots her head off during the
beginning of the weeklong Eid-e-Ghorbon trying to forget
all i am forced to remember razor wire nights Koochie boys
wearing desert faces speaking to me in all the languages
of hunger begging for gold thread i don't remember the
name of the particular dark Pashtun male or the color of
Zarah's wedding dress i try to forget her smile the way
blood creates its own art spraying the cake the gifts of sugar
bread honey spices prayer carpets scarves from her sisters i
remember your daily screams when i forgot and opened the
door to visitors in Peshawar forgetting always to wear my
chador i remind you that i am the same woman who raced
barefoot escaping the war rapes of sixty Russians behind
a hill in Wazir Akbu Khan i am the woman you danced
with beneath the stars in Kandahar the same astrologer
who meets your eyes in the bazaar i am every woman in
the snow covered streets of Ghazni or in Herat Province
lighting candles in search of Zarah's gold teeth i am the lost
bullet lodged in the wedding cake that the man with green
teeth serves to his new bride Fatima i will meet her in the
bathroom stalls next door to the blue mosque and pretend
i do not see her tap my market basket remove the muslin
cloth covering the fresh chicken dates onions potatoes
lemons drop my knife into the deep pockets of her riding
skirts our smiles whispering salaams it is the coldest night
without you and i am preparing a dinner for your return the
foods of our passionate longings lentil and bulgur patties
stuffed eggplant kasseri cheese my brother smuggles from
Turkey chicken pilaf raisin compote i spend hours shaving
oiling my skin soaking in frankincense ginger jasmine water
arrange rose petals throughout our bed sharpen candle
sticks that will light this night there is no more hashish guns
or knives only the wedding feast waiting.

parched lips for a legless dancer

i offer a body swept clean by hungry ghosts no manna
beneath this rock of flesh so sharp the horizon slices open
i grow two icy hearts for the torn pleasure that promises
attack hidden lotus flower mango scented fingers lick and
receive this night flowering appendage of would be flesh left
over dreams of war fossilized childhood white prayer worms
nibble stretch my dusty hips into a path winding through
starless valleys old women gather in a kitchen pray for rain
one less lynching one less daughter breeding in the weeds of
acres their hands cannot claim acres that name their bones
another winter in this land of cain where scars are bright
rules whip across your back where galvanized tin mirrors
flatter the bruises like the dishonest soul's smirking tearing at
its own likeness forgive us for we do not know how to kneel
the wind speaks that too is prayer my grandmother stands
with old women on a porch stained by shackled innocence
she works through the night building coffins listening to the
hymns of tiny devils she wolves dance beyond the dark hair
wet alive merges with the wood her fur-winged lover chants
a wrenching wounded hosanna sings praises to a legless
moon whore becomes forbidden night shapes feasts on
scissor-handed scorpions steals the lovely song of kindness
from a merciful divinity.

Inside a Jallalabad Mirage

Skeletons of olive trees become sisters swallowing rain
swallowing whispers shrouds masks illegitimate suicides
birthed by the intoxicated rage of jihad ghosts
searching for their shadows.

Sisters become tree tombs
disguise the unearthing of whispering crypts
provide night cover map geography.

Birthed by fire
these singed angels wail beyond *fajr*
slip out of ancient burqa stitches
fall through seven heavens.

Rattling ancient womb drums
into mourning message
they free imprisoned hair necks arms hands legs.

Wife of the olive grove
picks up wilted parchment of a face
never held to the light
gathers warrior bones of a drowned daughter.

Gathering ochre teeth dust from her feet
she offers olives as prayer sacrifice
blood payment.

The needles of a thousand jinn
dance above the heads
of these wailing tree women
who stretch themselves across the graves
of massacred virgins.

Carve new wombs with their breath
beneath the holiness of seven gates
dig for a ransomed dowry with their teeth
wait for a glimpse of The Beloved.

feeding the light
for aunt lilly
(who taught me how to see in the dark)

we risk ice storms postpone passionate death to swirl head
first beyond wise breathing lessons beyond crimson soaked
necks crushed knuckles and stinking birth skin all the way
down past gray fields chaste moons yet light so pregnant it
seeps across insolent skies too ashamed to name the dances
too ashamed to name the shaman who eats the jazz behind
iron doors praying for half notes that cure blindness cure
the bestial that lurks inside places troubles on the water one
tenor eyelash at a time reappearing at the bottom of a worn
out morning after cup of miles pharoah herbie ornette we
risk falling out of the well used belly the platinum engraved
womb that cherishes a right handed bass player clean blue
velvet shoes that keep nameless eyes waiting he has a way
of singing thick thighs apart in the middle of blazing duets
knows how to pull blossoms out of the ground through
february snow drifts feeds a bastard sky child nothing but
horn a wild child reading the book of the thousand nights
and a night blue velvet shoes can't keep a damn lie straight
in between identifying frozen crushed faces slaughtered for
whispering jazz slaughtered for smelling like jazz wooden
zulu spears silver coins wet feathers we risk losing our
sense of flight our gypsy hearts in search of jazz eating
shaman who serves holy bread with blues water his voice
slicing daylight feeding small pieces to all that is left of a
brown jungle girl whose bones smoke up every juke joint in
between here and all the places she died alone on alabaster
steps voice strangled by kisses prayers abandoned weeping
shaman cures her dreams pours billie sarah nina ella down
her throat horny hips thrust shatter shred blue velvet shoes
across the room a narrow mirror becomes a road and she

learns to fly straight through a glass sky she be music now she be night-fed she be forgiveness rupturing a worn out morning after cup of herself she be birthing remixing clocks calendars numbers maps her sweat sweet round midnight honey washing up onto a shore of seasons smelling like drums tasting like a flute of curry we risk night searching wanting to taste her skin.

blues for wounded laughter

i first saw him at the two skate for one rate tuesday night
skate party with cousin adele me in shimmering pastels
chocolate brown ski parka aunt frida talking bout adele you
need to get your cousin jade outta this house meet some
of them dread heads they nice men don't mean women
nothing but respect show good times all the time i twirl
with chaka khan purple beats the funk of earth wind and fire
every man the color of winter reminds me of other dances
other nights that have no place on calendars a lover a blues
tune stuck beneath my tongue an unholy night conjures
paul curly fro law student wet smile pleasures my ears but
hands like wood trying to tear history out of my womb
trying to drink past a stretch of night that abandons him
on his own shores of father mother prisoner buried alive
beneath diminishing light of his mothers eyes her sprawling
death the only sound he can hear when he lies awake in
my arms his hands needed to have their say strike the
hush in his fathers fist rearrange bones beneath my chest
write blood sonnets flunk bar exams cook up ceremony
of apology waiting for visitations of his mothers sprawling
death his fathers airborne fist i marched to his love his
fire his tears i marched to his mothers breathless gasp the
stack of broken bones bruised lips shifting wombs saved by
history that flowed through him paul turned the gun away
from me that night wrapped his pain in gun powder so blue
i thought his hands were breathing an echo that aroused his
mother loosened her screaming her ghost thighs quivering
receiving him back beyond a womb of silence tonight my
lungs yearn to forget the taste of broken glass yearn to
regret two years of standing holding my breath behind
shower curtains locked doors my feet have a plan of their
own teasing the ice tearing laughter out of my stitched

throat luther vandross making my hips rise wade through
around beneath couples caught up in their own illusions
he is skating beside me feet rooted like trees of his south
american forest smiling warrior polished hands so smooth
i can hear the rivers of his childhood his hands his heart's
wealth let me be your wind tonight his shoulders whisper
i answer yes to locks of hair already cruising my bones
we tango past stars past butterflies all the way to a path
of drums candles frankincense a house of plenty tongues
i make good on the prophecy of an elder lock out smells
blue gun smoke take back my nights honey smeared poetry
stained dawns tonight i will not be afraid to reach over close
the window light a fire.

brothers with dreadlocks will kill you too

we sat glazed translucent slicing our love into thick rings
like onions for stew or soup we pretended we weren't
earthbound king queen of too many dramas that left me
wandering alone picking flowers that had no smell whose
blossoms did not die wilt bleed beneath strangulations
we grew fond of the toxins breeding under our pillows
confessions that shake hair skin loose shed memories like
childhood diseases i am not a man to use my hands for
anything but pleasure art praise i will not walk these streets
for a job it always led back to this conversation money for
the rent the electricity i wanted to walk with him all the
way to his country to his blind grandmother her herd of
goats his uncles backs scorched in banana fields i wanted to
run with him in a field of blossoms that would bend under
our feet but he could not go back to the ghosts that had
learned how to pick the locks on his grandmothers doors
instead they followed learned the languages of a thousand
borders they watch us from the bowl of mangoes crawl
through our dirty laundry scratch their teeth on the last fifty
dollar hidden beneath my socks a feast of blood he wrote
across the mirrors throughout the house a feast of words
red pink orange blush gold lipsticks broken smeared listen
to me his eyes cried my mouth is out of order my spirit
drags me rises to the top of the ceiling a room of pleasure
i discover a new cobalt in the moroccan rugs reflections
of my still hands mesmerize inlaid mirrors turkish tea trays
overturned wooden bracelets dangling silver bells sparkling
light witness red silk bedspread waiting for my hair to spill
spread antique sari curtains stained by my blood books
journals prayer beads a womb field of lavender his dreads
soaking my blood his fingers removing the pearl necklace
from the carved bedpost a gift for the daughter i will

never meet now as his feet explode inside his head his pee rattling like yellow rain my last breath finds a hole inside his coat pocket i crawl inside listen to his heart write beat escape wipe the splattered blood from his undying love confession our lips remember this unspoken death our home remembers window sills of lavender peasant bread papaya salsa mint baths rosemary mornings two mounds of red earth where elders wail stoop to listen to the crone who sells fish in the market her breath stinking truth into chastising i no cry for the young lions what you mean you think him no kill she.

digging for grandmothers

"...the things that we love tell us what we are."
Thomas Merton

the house is sunday silent the usual visitation finches
hovering beyond the open window flirting with stray
hummingbirds aroused by orange lantana prostrating fertile
rosemary in pitch with flowering lavender sunlit foreplay
interrupt holiness

never sweep your hair into the wind

i mistake my grandmother's voice for the sound of morning
soft thin liquid like her hands fertile iroquois hopi cherokee
red hands that wrestle capture swallow hold light hostage
inside her belly teaching daughters granddaughters how to
weave water into baskets

it is best to gather thunder on your knees

apprentice to wind and river forging centuries of breath into
wet carolina clay
her pots jars bowls burial urns speak with swirling bear ribs
turtle tracks wolf tongues
at my birthing she offered me to the water dervishes in
hope of ransoming a wind she could not name the house
listens with me for the sound of crawling feathers

only your feet can teach you
that the sound of earth will keep you walking upright

the disappearance of somersaulting finches paralysis of the
air signal her arrival

i gather vials of jasmine sandalwood sage cedar
from the fireplace
reminding me ascension requires aloe lavender amber
white rose myrrh
this house sighs remembers to breathe i loosen long silver
braids step outside

don't make a fist when you hold the fire's tail

my feet sing loud against a selfish earth denying me first
embrace red wings beneath crone soles roots grasses vines
gather creating lush primal maps kneeling beneath canopy
of iron stone feathers four generations of hydrangeas bow
ceremoniously i try to out sing the wind

ask permission of the plants before you cut them

i am your daughter harbinger to bone totems bottle trees
moss mounds cypress arbors
islands of sea glass…teach me to dance across a ceiling of red

for amiri baraka

I come from a black box that spoon-fed me your words one
drop at a time choking me on some leroi jones words like
dat have to be sliced off real thin too much going through
your ears too fast like a baby seal my tongue was always
alert erect ready for the next drop my mama didn't put
no sugar at the bottom of the spoon either i come from
cotton walls and factory furniture plastic fruit and singing
vines from vintage to postmodern and all the way back
your poems have residence here on wooden bench swings
scarred mahogany dining room tables that hush and seal
all the scratched in stories your poems live in china closets
beside county fair prizes salt boxes porcelain dolls we
listened read screamed your words across this *amerikkka*
from bootleg alleys bow legged hollows snaggle-tooth
harbors i was one of those teens in jeans more raggedy
than a can of kraut feasting on poem pimps with sharkskin
feet monogrammed teeth hiding their gun power in back
yard family reunion ice chests we hollered your words
baby poets searching for just the right piece of glass wood
cement to chew on we screamed your poems all across this
amerikkka i come from argo starch red clay eating women
i come from wizards deacons hootcie hustlers *silver bullet*
mason dixie illegitimacy shotgun weddings talking bottle
trees secrets of the whore secrets of the midwife secrets of
the daughter i come from men whose eyes were lost in the
japanese theater traded for snow traded for bread ash paper
that's why i need to be spoon-fed your iron soup i come
from sardines saltines a pinch of sugar in the beans a pinch
of glass in the sugar fish frys in the woods blood stained
bibles i come from pressed dollars and just enough pennies
for the tooth fairy and still i found your words *the toilet the
duthchman dante's hell* i found them from the cousin just
back from *nam* who was drowning in *hot buttered soul last*

poets earth wind and fire hassan roland kirk forest flower in
between nods from a jones not related to you *leroi jones*
under a sweating tree i found your words from that sista
they told me to stay away from who just showed up one
day in my aunt's living room she wasn't homeless she just
didn't have a bed i found you in the corners of all the *jersey*
cousins daddies' trunks every summer trading seersucker
for banlon polyester trading *johnny walker* for *white lightning*
you smeared your frothy funk in the darkest corners of juke
joints barber shops deacon corners you became amazing
grace in thunder studded ditches high rolling poker parties
but i found you i found you i found you on the top of
refrigerators in market baskets apron pockets trumpet cases
i dropped your words in that big mud puddle between " miss
so and so" and "whatcha ma call hers" house on my way to
babysit toothless twins drying your words out like grandma
dried apples peaches cherries on the tin top well we
screamed your words all across *amerikkka* from screened
porches swinging tires sweating rooftops we screamed we
screamed we screamed cause we had never found words
like these before never found words like these before never
found words like these before i found my ice my glass my
wood my nail the something my poet teeth needed to chew
on barefoot south summer hair gal getting grown too slow
wading in duck ponds crawling through windows that have
forgotten how to lock lock lock i be the teen child nursing
your poems from a big titty woman tree practicing how to
burn in the dark i be seven drunk crows bearing down on
amerikkka's carrion licking stink and loving this stink from
the bones from the bones from the bones you showed me
how to shoot words out of the sky hunt them down under
rocks make a pen slingshot arrow fire.

an eclipse of skin

i

the blood was the calling

ii

ancient spirits
gather beneath erect feet
cry an ancestral anointment
kiss torn torso
restitch face to smile

iii

splintered hands
hold death songs
one breath crawling towards light

iv

hidden in every finger joint
hidden between shoulder and neck
hidden between heart and rib

v

yo hair is in my drink missus sarah
go ahead and move it william
you know you don't want to drink my hair
do you william?

vi

*$20 Reward…Ranaway from the subscriber, after asking my
wife, a white Christian clean woman for a drink of wata, and
then touching her apron on the 22nd December last. My nigga,
William, baptized by my pappy, is age about 23 years. He is a
shiny black, lean built with large limbs, long fingers, he is hung
like a race horse. He has unusually small feet for a nigga and
missing the toe next to his great toe on his left foot. It has been
mashed off. I will pay the above reward on his delivery or proof
of his hanging in any nearby county.*
James R. Wood
February 6. 1844

vii

masa hung my william
had him hung from the chinaberry tree
same tree my william plant for masa
when william was just a child
masa make me and my baby liza watch
   from the kitchen
liza my child and massa child too
i don't cry
liza don't cry
she mo irish than masa
one day liza remember this day
remember what huh pappy done
one day liza remember missus sarah
sitting in the parlor with her sistah emma
drinking elderberry wine
complaining bout how william blood gone kill
   the grass

viii

masa had him hung
passed out cigars and cups of peach brandy
made me suck him off in the kitchen
in front of aunt sue
making apple fritters

ix

aunt sue spoke to the apples
aunt sue spoke to the sugar
aunt sue spoke to the fire

x

the trees
the ground
the wind
remember
in all the languages
of storm

xi

sky black this morning liza
black like masa blood up yonder
black like missus scalp
rolling off the bed

xii

morning sky black
seven crows circle
gather blood from ground
paint clouds red
perch atop chinaberry tree
swallow light

Jaki Shelton Green is a poet, creativity coach, teacher, and cultural activist. Her books include *Dead on Arrival, Dead on Arrival and New Poems, Conjure Blues, singing a tree into dance*, and *breath of the song*. The recipient of many awards, she was recently inducted into the North Carolina Literary Hall of Fame. She lives in Mebane, North Carolina.